I0845315
Kitty Newbold

This book is dedicated to all the young explorers who are curious about the wonders of the ocean.

Just like the majestic sea turtles, may you always find your way home, learn from the world around you, and understand the importance of protecting the places we love.

Let the turtles' journey inspire you to be brave, kind, and caring, both in your adventures and in life.

The sun shimmered through the reef as Finley darted around, his yellow fins sparkling in the water.

"Where are you going so fast?"

Tess giggled, her emerald-green shell glinting in the light.

"Guess what?" Tess said, a smile in her voice. "It's time for the great turtle migration!"

Finley stopped mid-swim.

"Migration? What's that?"

"It's the journey we turtles take every year," Tess explained.

"We travel far across the ocean to lay our eggs."

Finley's eyes widened with excitement.

"Can I come with you?
I've never traveled so far!"

Tess grinned. "Of course!
We can explore new places together."

With the reef disappearing behind them,
Tess and Finley swam side by side, heading
into the open ocean.

The waves were calm, and the sea
stretched endlessly ahead of them.

"I can't believe we're finally doing this!"
Finley exclaimed, his eyes wide with
excitement.

They weaved through a towering forest of seaweed, the long fronds swaying gently in the current.

Colorful fish darted in and out of the greenery, playing their own game of hide and seek.

"This place is amazing!" Finley said, twirling in circles.

Tess smiled, her heart calm and content.

A group of dolphins appeared, leaping and twirling out of the water.

Their squeaks echoed playfully, inviting Finley and Tess to join in.

"Think you can keep up?" one dolphin teased with a grin.

"Let's go!" Finley laughed,
"We'll swim faster to keep up!"

After hours of swimming, Tess led them to a quiet sea cave where glowing creatures lit up the walls like tiny stars in the water.

"We can rest here for a while," Tess said, her voice soft.

Finley looked around in awe, the soft lights dancing in his bright eyes.

As they rested, Finley asked, "Tess, why do turtles make this long journey every year?"

Tess smiled. "We sea turtles return to the same beaches where we were born, like here in the Florida Keys, to lay our eggs.

It's part of our life cycle, and it helps bring new turtles into the world."

"So most turtles come back to where they started, just like you?" Finley asked.

Tess nodded. "Yes, it connects us to our past and makes sure future turtles have a place to call home."

As they swam deeper, the water grew darker, and large manta rays glided gracefully overhead like underwater birds.

Beneath them, a group of vibrant sea slugs crawled along the ocean floor, their colors swirling like tiny rainbows.

"Look at them!" Finley whispered in awe. "They're like jewels of the sea!"

"The deep ocean has many wonders," Tess said with admiration.

They swam until they spotted a giant sea turtle resting on a rock.

His shell was covered in barnacles, and his eyes were calm and wise.

"Welcome, young travelers," the elder turtle said in a deep voice.

"We are migrating with the other sea turtles!" Tess excitedly said.

The elder turtle replied, "The ocean is vast, but you are strong. Respect the sea, and it will guide you on your journey."

Tess and Finley were grateful for the elder's words of wisdom.

As they swam further, the water began to churn, and dark clouds rolled overhead.

Tess looked up, her eyes narrowing. "A storm is coming," she said, her voice calm but serious.

Finley's heart raced. "What do we do?"

"Stay close to me, Finley.

We'll find shelter," Tess replied, guiding him through the growing waves.

The sky darkened, and the ocean roared.

Waves crashed around them, pushing
Finley and Tess in every direction.

Thunder rumbled through the water, and
lightning flickered above.

"Hold on!" Tess called over the roaring sea,
her flippers working hard to stay
in front of Finley.

A huge wave pulled Finley away, sweeping him into the swirling waters.

"Tess!" he shouted, fear gripping him.

But before he could panic, Tess was there.

She grabbed him with her strong jaws and pulled him toward a rocky outcropping, where they huddled safely from the storm.

"I've got you," Tess whispered, her heart still pounding.

As the storm passed, the sea became calm once again.

The clouds parted, revealing a bright blue sky.

A beautiful rainbow stretched across the horizon; its glorious colors were shimmering in the water below.

"We made it," Finley said with a sigh of relief, his fins still trembling.

"We did it together," Tess replied with a gentle smile.

Finally, they reached the island where hundreds of sea turtles were gathered on the sandy shore.

The beach glittered under the warm sun, and the soft sound of waves filled the air.

"This is it," Tess said, her voice full of wonder. "The place where we lay our eggs."

Finley watched in amazement as the turtles slowly made their way up the beach.

Tess and Finley marveled as the adult turtles made their way up to the beach.

The sand sparkled in the sunlight as each turtle found a special place
to lay their eggs.

"One day, I'll be part of this too," Tess whispered to Finley.

Finley nodded, his eyes wide with wonder.

"It's amazing how they all come back to this same place."

After watching the turtles for a while, Tess and Finley, with the sun glistening on the water, began their journey home.

"We've learned so much," Finley said, swimming alongside Tess.

Together, they swam back to their reef, where their friends awaited, their hearts brimming with new wisdom and excitement for the adventures still to come.

Scan and look for more
undersea adventures!

If you enjoyed this book,
it would mean the world
to us if you could leave
an honest review ...

Scan the code to join
Kitty's List, and never
miss an update!

RED
LIGHT GREEN
BROWN
CRAYON
TURQUOISE

www.ingramcontent.com/pod-product-compliance
Lightning Source LLC
Chambersburg PA
CBHW040159240726
48664CB00002B/766